Mattison,

Graduation isn't [the end of a] tough journey. It [is the beginning] of a beautiful one! May God bless you along the way.

Congratulations!
The Amasons

For _____

From _____

Date _____

Don't abandon wisdom, and she will watch over you; love her, and she will guard you. Wisdom is supreme—so get wisdom. And whatever else you get, get understanding.
~ Proverbs 4:6–7

Bible promises

you've just graduated, and life as
you've known it will never be the same. You'll be
faced with new and wonderful opportunities
—as well as many new challenges. This is for
you . . . to read, to pray, to meditate, to equip,
to teach, to live . . . for the
Graduate

KAREN MOORE

Bible promises

you've just graduated, and life as you've known it will never be the same. You'll be faced with new and wonderful opportunities —as well as many new challenges. This is for you . . . to read, to pray, to meditate, to equip, to teach, to live . . .

for the Graduate

PUBLISHING GROUP

www.BHPublishingGroup.com

NASHVILLE, TENNESSEE

Copyright © 2014 by B&H Publishing Group

All rights reserved.

Printed in China

978-1-4336-8219-3

Published by B&H Publishing Group, Nashville, Tennessee

Dewey Decimal Classification: 242.643

Subject Heading: CHRISTIAN LIFE \ DEVOTIONAL
LITERATURE \ STUDENTS

Quotes taken from:

The New Encyclopedia of Christian Quotations

Published by Baker Books

©2000 John Hunt Publishing Ltd.

P.O. Box 6287, Grand Rapids, MI 49516-6287

2 3 4 5 6 7 8 • 18 17 16 15 14

Contents

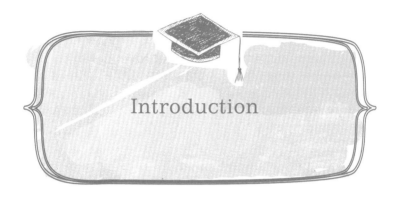

Introduction

A graduation celebrates beginnings and endings. Some time ago, you set a goal to earn a degree, a particular level of formal education. You had to focus right from the beginning on what you hoped to achieve at the end.

You succeeded and now the future stands before you. It's time to reflect on how far you've come and the work it took to get there. From here, you'll set new goals. Perhaps you'll choose to get a more advanced degree. Perhaps you'll simply begin a new life out in the world. Either way, you will take another leap of faith and start all over again.

The blessing in all of this is that you've picked up some clues about what you have to do to make things happen and you've begun to understand that what you do matters. It matters to you, to your family, and to God.

Look at these promises of God for your life and know that He has a great plan for you, a plan that brings hope and a future. The more you communicate with Him, the more you walk with Him, the more you'll enjoy each new step you take.

May God shine His light on your life and on your dreams as you begin . . . again!

Karen Moore

1

It's a Whole New World for You!

The next moment is as much beyond our grasp, and as much in God's care, as that a hundred years away. Concern for the next minute is just as foolish as concern for a day in the next thousand years. In neither can we do anything, in both, God is doing everything. ~ C. S. Lewis

As you step out into a whole new world, uncertain yet of its direction or design, it helps to know that you are not walking alone. The One who knew you even before you were born knew this day would come and is already preparing the way for all you are meant to achieve. God has always been in your life and will be there for the long haul.

Starting over can seem scary. It can feel like you're on your own no matter how many well-wishers surround you. After all, you're the one who has to do the work and create the dream. In a world as changing and sometimes volatile as this one, you will have to prepare yourself, seeking God's guidance for all you do. Together, you will create a life that is beyond your imagination. Your new journey will not always be easy and you will not always succeed, but you will always have a place to go for comfort, hope, and replenishment. Take a look at how you know God is walking beside you.

Scripture to Guide You

My Stronghold

> The LORD is my light and my salvation—
> whom should I fear? The LORD is the
> stronghold of my life—of whom should I
> be afraid? ~ Psalm 27:1

Perfect Peace

> You will keep the mind that is dependent
> on You in perfect peace, for it is trusting
> in You. ~ Isaiah 26:3

God's Faithfulness

> LORD, Your faithful love reaches to
> heaven, Your faithfulness to the clouds.

Your righteousness is like the highest mountains; Your judgments, like the deepest sea. LORD, You preserve man and beast. God, Your faithful love is so valuable that people take refuge in the shadow of Your wings. They are filled from the abundance of Your house; You let them drink from Your refreshing stream, for with You is life's fountain. In Your light we will see light.
~ Psalm 36:5–9

God's Deliverance

The righteous cry out, and the LORD hears, and delivers them from all their troubles. The LORD is near the broken-hearted; He saves those crushed in spirit.

Many adversities come to the one who is righteous, but the LORD delivers him from them all. ~ Psalm 34:17–19

God's Lead

This is what the LORD, your Redeemer, the Holy One of Israel says: "I am Yahweh your God, who teaches you for your benefit, who leads you in the way you should go." ~ Isaiah 48:17

5

Alpha and Omega

I am the Alpha and the Omega, the First and the Last, the Beginning and the End. ~ Revelation 22:13

He Will Not Forsake You

He will not leave you, destroy you, or forget the covenant with your fathers that He swore to them by oath, because the LORD your GOD is a compassionate God. ~ Deuteronomy 4:31

The Lord Is With You

"Haven't I commanded you: be strong and courageous? Do not be afraid or discouraged, for the LORD your God is with you wherever you go." ~ Joshua 1:9

The Lord Is Near

The LORD is near all who call out to Him, all who call out to Him with integrity. ~ Psalm 145:18

My Spirit Is With You

"This is the promise I made to you when you came out of Egypt, and My Spirit is present among you; don't be afraid."
~ Haggai 2:5

He Is Not Far Away

He did this so they might seek God, and perhaps they might reach out and find Him, though He is not far from each one of us. ~ Acts 17:27

The Lord Is at Hand

Let your graciousness be known to everyone. The Lord is near.
~ Philippians 4:5

God Is Your Shield

Every word of God is pure; He is a shield to those who take refuge in Him.
~ Proverbs 30:5

Quotes to Encourage You

The Bible is one of the greatest blessings bestowed by God on the children of men. It has God for its author, salvation for its end, and truth without any mixture for its matter. It is all pure, all sincere; nothing too much; nothing too little. ~ John Locke

If you abandon all restraint, carry your wishes to their furthest limits, open your heart boundlessly, there is not a single moment when you will not find all you could possibly desire. The present moment holds infinite riches beyond your wildest dreams. ~ Jean-Pierre de Caussade

I no longer believe that God is up there, and I do not believe that God is only within me, and I do not believe that God is merely out there in history. I think we are actually in God at all times. ~ Sister Madonna Kolbenschlag

One of the most powerful concepts, one which is a sure cure for lack of confidence, is the thought that God is with you and helping you. This is one of the simplest teachings in religion, namely, that Almighty God will be your companion, will stand by you, help you, and see you through. No other idea is so powerful in developing self-confidence as this simple belief when practiced. To practice it, simply affirm "God is with me; God is helping me; God is guiding me." Spend several minutes each day visualizing his presence. Then practice believing that affirmation. ~ Norman Vincent Peale

Even if I knew that tomorrow the world would go to pieces, I would still plant my apple tree. ~ Martin Luther

Never be afraid to trust an unknown future to a known God. ~ Corrie Ten

Prayer

Lord, there is nothing that instills confidence like trusting and believing in Your presence in my life. Help me to know that You are always at my side and that You are going before me, preparing the way for all You want me to become and to accomplish. You hold the plans for my life in Your hand. Thank You for guiding me each step of the way. Amen.

2

Creating Community—
Growing, Sharing, Believing!

Christ has no body now on earth but yours; yours are the only
hands with which he can do his work, yours are the only feet
with which he can go about the world, yours are the only eyes
through which his compassion can shine forth upon a troubled
world. Christ has no body now on earth but yours.
~ Teresa of Avila

Now that you've graduated, it's likely that you could
find yourself in a new location, perhaps going to a school
in a different city from where you were, or going to a
new job. For a variety of reasons, whether now or later
you may find yourself in all new surroundings. Once
you have gotten reestablished in your new community,
you may find yourself seeking ways to connect and truly

11

settle in. One of the best ways to achieve a sense of community is by offering your service to others.

Sometimes we put the idea of service on the same back burner as diet and exercise. We think it's a good idea, but something we'll do later. The trouble with that approach is that the needs are out there today. What if you decided instead to give God your availability? What if you let Him know that on Tuesdays at 3:00 you could be free to volunteer at a nearby shelter or a food pantry? You would be answering a call and you would be acting as the hands, feet, and heart of God for the people in your neighborhood. When you offer God your time, He equips you for the task and gives you the opportunity. You will never run out of work, never be laid off, and never be told your service is not needed.

Consider your talents and abilities. How can you use them to serve others? How can you be God's hands and feet for your friends and the people in your community? It's good to talk about serving. It's better to serve!

Scripture to Guide You

Good to Great!

> The greatest among you will be your servant. Whoever exalts himself will be humbled, and whoever humbles himself will be exalted. ~ Matthew 23:11–12

Working for the Lord

Therefore, my dear brothers, be steadfast, immovable, always excelling in the Lord's work, knowing that your labor in the Lord is not in vain. ~ 1 Corinthians 15:58

Finding the Strength to Serve

If anyone speaks, it should be as one who speaks God's words; if anyone serves, it should be from the strength God provides, so that God may be glorified through Jesus Christ in everything. To Him belong the glory and the power forever and ever. Amen. ~ 1 Peter 4:11

Imitate God

Therefore, be imitators of God, as dearly loved children. ~ Ephesians 5:1

What It Means to Be Wise

Better is a poor but wise youth than an old but foolish king who no longer pays attention to warnings. ~ Ecclesiastes 4:13

No One Lives to Himself

> For none of us lives to himself, and no one dies to himself. ~ Romans 14:7

Knowledgeable Shepherds

> "Return, you faithless children"—this is the LORD's declaration—"for I am your master, and I will take you, one from a city and two from a family, and I will bring you to Zion. I will give you shepherds who are loyal to Me, and they will shepherd you with knowledge and skill." ~ Jeremiah 3:14–15

Your Gifts to Serve

> Based on the gift each one has received, use it to serve others, as good managers of the varied grace of God. If anyone speaks, it should be as one who speaks God's words; if anyone serves, it should be from the strength God provides, so that God may be glorified through Jesus Christ in everything. To Him belong the glory and the power forever and ever. Amen. ~ 1 Peter 4:10–11

Be an Example

Let no one despise your youth; instead, you should be an example to the believers in speech, in conduct, in love, in faith, in purity. ~ 1 Timothy 4:12

Being of One Body

Now as we have many parts in one body, and all the parts do not have the same function, in the same way we who are many are one body in Christ and individually members of one another. ~ Romans 12:4–5

Be a Good Servant

It must not be like that among you. On the contrary, whoever wants to become great among you must be your servant, and whoever wants to be first among you must be your slave; just as the Son of Man did not come to be served, but to serve, and to give His life—a ransom for many. ~ Matthew 20:26–28

The Service of Shirts and Shoes

> He replied to them, "The one who has two shirts must share with someone who has none, and the one who has food must do the same." ~ Luke 3:11

Quotes to Encourage You

Give to people for whom this world is hard and bad the belief that there is a better life made for them. Scatter Gospels among the villages, a Bible for every cottage.
~ Victor Hugo

The Lord doesn't ask about your ability, only your availability; and, if you prove your dependability, the Lord will increase your capability. ~ Author Unknown

To give real service you must add something which cannot be bought or measured with money, and that is sincerity and integrity. ~ Donald A. Adams

In the time we have it is surely our duty to do all the good we can to all the people we can in all the ways we can. ~ William Barclay

We are not built for ourselves, but for God. Not for service for God, but FOR God. ~ Oswald Chambers

*If I can stop one heart from breaking,
I shall not live in vain;
If I can ease one life the aching,
Or cool one pain,
Or help one fainting robin
Unto his nest again,
I shall not live in vain. ~ Emily Dickinson*

17

Every successful business in the world is in existence because its founder recognized in a problem or need an opportunity to be of service to others. Every problem or need in your life is in reality an opportunity to call forth inner resources of wisdom, love, strength, and ability. ~ J. Sig Paulson

I don't know what your destiny will be, but one thing I know, the only ones among you who will be really happy are those who have sought and found how to serve.
~ Albert Schweitzer

Prayer

Lord, You know the needs of those around me. You know my abilities and capabilities. Strengthen my spirit and lead me in service to those who are dear to my heart and those who are dear to Your heart. Grant me wisdom as I seek ways to connect with others in my work and community. Amen.

3

Continuing Education for Your Soul

As a student, you were taught skills and given tools to help you consider things wisely and to reason them out to the best conclusions. A willingness to seek wise solutions to life's troubles will serve you well. However, reason only offers you half of the equation.

John Donne said, "Reason is our soul's left hand, faith her right." It's great to be a reasonable person, able to seek and accept advice and move forward with confidence. The problem is that at one time or another, reason will fail you. Reason will not have the answers to the circumstances in which you find yourself.

The blessing then is that faith steps in. Faith reaches out to you and draws you into the inner circle of God's grace, mercy, and peace. Faith helps you overcome obstacles, comforts you in heartbreak, and creates a safe place for you to start again. Faith is your strongest ally.

As you begin a new course for your life, be sure to take both reason and faith along. Open your heart to God and He will equip you in every way. The education of your soul is a continuing journey and you are not alone. Step out in faith and become all you were meant to be.

Scripture to Guide You

Growing Up

> My little children, I am writing you these things so that you may not sin. But if anyone does sin, we have an advocate with the Father—Jesus Christ the Righteous One. He Himself is the propitiation for our sins, and not only for ours, but also for those of the whole world. ~ 1 John 2:1–2

God Called You

> But we must always thank God for you, brothers loved by the Lord, because from the beginning God has chosen you for salvation through sanctification by the Spirit and through belief in the truth. He called you to this through

our gospel, so that you might obtain the glory of our Lord Jesus Christ.
~ 2 Thessalonians 2:13–14

Faith's Foundation

Jesus told him, "I am the way, the truth, and the life. No one comes to the Father except through Me." ~ John 14:6

For God So Loved You

"For God loved the world in this way: He gave His One and Only Son, so that everyone who believes in Him will not perish but have eternal life." ~ John 3:16

Walking by the Spirit

Therefore, no condemnation now exists for those in Christ Jesus, because the Spirit's law of life in Christ Jesus has set you free from the law of sin and of death. What the law could not do since it was limited by the flesh, God did. He condemned sin in the flesh by sending His own Son in flesh like ours under sin's domain, and as a sin offering, in order that the law's requirement would be accomplished in us who do not walk according to the flesh but according to the Spirit. ~ Romans 8:1–4

What Feeds Us

"My food is to do the will of Him who sent Me and to finish His work," Jesus told them. ~ John 4:34

Setting New Goals

More than that, I also consider everything to be a loss in view of the surpassing value of knowing Christ Jesus my Lord. Because of Him I have suffered the loss of all things and consider them filth, so that I may gain Christ and be found in Him, not having a righteousness of my own from the law, but one that is through faith in Christ—the righteousness from God based on faith. My goal is to know Him and the power of His resurrection and the fellowship of His sufferings, being conformed to His death, assuming that I will somehow reach the resurrection from among the dead. ~ Philippians 3:8–11

Carry Each Other's Burdens

Carry one another's burdens; in this way you will fulfill the law of Christ. For if anyone considers himself to be something when he is nothing, he deceives himself. ~ Galatians 6:2–3

Teach Me Lord!

Teach me, LORD, the meaning of Your statutes, and I will always keep them.

Help me understand Your instruction, and I will obey it and follow it with all my heart.

Help me stay on the path of Your commands, for I take pleasure in it.

Turn my heart to Your decrees and not to material gain.

Turn my eyes from looking at what is worthless; give me life in Your ways.

Confirm what You said to Your servant, for it produces reverence for You.

Turn away the disgrace I dread; indeed, Your judgments are good.

How I long for Your precepts! Give me life through Your righteousness.
~ Psalm 119:33–40

The Beatitudes

Then looking up at His disciples, He said:

"You who are poor are blessed, because the kingdom of God is yours.

"You who are now hungry are blessed, because you will be filled. You who now weep are blessed, because you will laugh. You are blessed when people hate you, when they exclude you, insult you, and slander your name as evil because of the Son of Man.

"Rejoice in that day and leap for joy! Take note—your reward is great in heaven, for this is the way their ancestors used to treat the prophets.

"But woe to you who are rich, for you have received your comfort. Woe to you who are now full, for you will be hungry. Woe to you who are now laughing, for you will mourn and weep.

"Woe to you when all people speak well of you, for this is the way their ancestors used to treat the false prophets." ~ Luke 6:20–26

Be of Good Courage

Be strong and courageous, all you who put your hope in the LORD. ~ Psalm 31:24

Your Strength

For the LORD GOD, the Holy One of Israel, has said: "You will be delivered by returning and resting; your strength will lie in quiet confidence. But you are not willing." ~ Isaiah 30:15

Mustard Seed Faith

"Because of your little faith," He told them. "For I assure you: If you have faith the size of a mustard seed, you will tell this mountain, 'Move from here to there,' and it will move. Nothing will be impossible for you." ~ Matthew 17:20

Moving Mountains

Jesus answered them, "I assure you: If you have faith and do not doubt, you will not only do what was done to the fig tree, but even if you tell this mountain, 'Be lifted up and thrown into the sea,' it will be done." ~ Matthew 21:21

What Faith Is All About

> Now faith is the reality of what is hoped
> for, the proof of what is not seen.
> ~ Hebrews 11:1

Faith and Knowledge

> For this very reason, make every effort
> to supplement your faith with goodness,
> goodness with knowledge. ~ 2 Peter 1:5

Quotes to Encourage You

Since grace does not scrap nature, but brings it to
perfection, so also natural reason should assist faith as
the natural bent of the will leads to charity.
~ Thomas Aquinas

There is difficulty about disagreeing with God.
He is the source from which all your reasoning
power comes. ~ C. S. Lewis

Human reason cannot begin to answer the great questions as to what God is in himself, and what he is in relation to us. ~ John Calvin

The ultimate purpose of reason is to bring us to a place where we can see that there is a limit to reason. ~ Blaise Pascal

Reason is the greatest enemy faith has: it never comes to the aid of spiritual things, but-more frequently than not—struggles against the divine Word, treating with contempt all that emanates from God. ~ Martin Luther

As we begin to focus upon God the things of the spirit will take shape before our inner eyes. Obedience to the word of Christ will bring an inward revelation of the Godhead. It will give acute perception enabling us to see God even as is promised to the pure in heart. A new God-consciousness will seize upon us and we shall begin to taste and hear and inwardly feel the God who is our life and our all. There will be seen the constant shining light that lights every human being who comes into the world. ~ A. W. Tozer (adapted)

Our faith comes in moments. Yet there is a depth to those brief moments which constrains us to ascribe more reality to them than to all other experiences. ~ Emerson

Take the first step in faith. You don't have to see the whole staircase, just take the first step. ~ Martin Luther King Jr.

If God promises something, then faith must fight a long and bitter fight, for reason or the flesh judges that God's promises are impossible. Therefore faith must battle against reason and its doubts. ~ Martin Luther

Trust the past to God's mercy, the present to God's love and the future to God's providence.
~ *Augustine of Hippo*

Amid trails hard, temptations strong, and troubles constant, true faith is persevering faith.
~ *Author Unknown.*

Prayer

Lord, thank You that human wisdom and reason are not the foundations of this world. Thank You that the learnings and the education built on theories and ideas are not the things that make the greatest difference in my heart and spirit. Knowing You and Your love is not a question of reason for me, but a matter of the heart and for that I am eternally grateful. Amen.

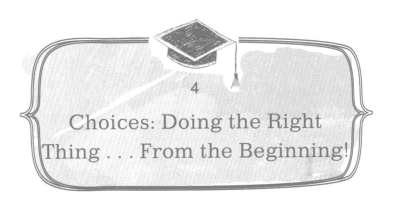

4

Choices: Doing the Right Thing . . . From the Beginning!

One's philosophy is not best expressed in words; it is expressed in the choices one makes. In the long run, we shape our lives and we shape ourselves. The process never ends until we die. And the choices we make are ultimately our responsibility.
~ Eleanor Roosevelt

You've lived long enough by now to have made some fabulous life choices and perhaps a few lousy ones. When we make good choices, we like to take the credit for them. When we make bad choices, we like to imagine that it's someone else's fault.

The above quote from Eleanor Roosevelt is a good reminder that we are ultimately responsible for the direction of our lives, based on the choices we make. If that's the case, it's important for you to consider carefully the kinds of choices you'll make. Every choice is followed by a result, sometimes even a consequence, and with God's help and grace, better choices can be made.

God knows the desires of your heart and wants you to succeed. He dreams of a better life for you. He knows all that you can be and is pleased with what He sees in you. How can you measure up to His vision of you then? How can you start today to make better choices for your life?

No matter where you've been, no matter how many unfortunate choices you may have made, God beckons you to try again. He calls you to draw closer to His side so that He can give you some clear instruction for your life. His Word is written in your hearts and has been set down in a manual for you to follow. Go to His textbook any time you need greater wisdom. It's a matter of continuing your education. You were designed for brilliance and it all begins with making good choices.

Scripture to Guide You

Renew Your Mind

> Do not be conformed to this age, but
> be transformed by the renewing of your
> mind, so that you may discern what is the
> good, pleasing, and perfect will of God.
> ~ Romans 12:2

Living Water

> On the last and most important day of
> the festival, Jesus stood up and cried out,
> "If anyone is thirsty, he should come to
> Me and drink! The one who believes in
> Me, as the Scripture has said, will have
> streams of living water flow from deep
> within him." ~ John 7:37–38

A New Mind Set

> You took off your former way of life,
> the old self that is corrupted by deceit-
> ful desires; you are being renewed in the
> spirit of your minds; you put on the new
> self, the one created according to God's
> likeness in righteousness and purity of
> the truth. ~ Ephesians 4:22–24

He Began a Good Work in You

> I am sure of this, that He who started
> a good work in you will carry it on to
> completion until the day of Christ Jesus.
> ~ Philippians 1:6

Strengthened to Make Good Choices

I pray that He may grant you, according to the riches of His glory, to be strengthened with power in the inner man through His Spirit, and that the Messiah may dwell in your hearts through faith. I pray that you, being rooted and firmly established in love, may be able to comprehend with all the saints what is the length and width, height and depth of God's love, and to know the Messiah's love that surpasses knowledge, so you may be filled with all the fullness of God.

Now to Him who is able to do above and beyond all that we ask or think according to the power that works in us— to Him be glory in the church and in Christ Jesus to all generations, forever and ever. Amen. ~ Ephesians 3:16–21

God's Armor

Put on the full armor of God so that you can stand against the tactics of the Devil. For our battle is not against flesh and blood, but against the rulers, against the authorities, against the world powers of this darkness, against the spiritual forces of evil in the heavens. This is why you must take up the full armor of God, so that you may be able to resist in the evil day, and having prepared everything, to take your stand. ~ Ephesians 6:11–13

Choose Life

I call heaven and earth as witnesses against you today that I have set before you life and death, blessing and curse. Choose life so that you and your descendants may live. ~ Deuteronomy 30:19

Choose to Serve the Lord

"But if it doesn't please you to worship Yahweh, choose for yourselves today the one you will worship: the gods your fathers worshiped beyond the Euphrates River or the gods of the Amorites in whose land you are living. As for me and my family, we will worship Yahweh." ~ Joshua 24:15

God Chose You

You did not choose Me, but I chose you. I appointed you that you should go out

and produce fruit and that your fruit
should remain, so that whatever you ask
the Father in My name, He will give you.
~ John 15:16

Use Good Judgment

Let us judge for ourselves what is right;
let us decide together what is good.
~ Job 34:4

Known By What You Do

So you'll recognize them by their fruit.
~ Matthew 7:20

Life or Death Choice

Then Jesus said to His disciples, "If
anyone wants to come with Me, he must
deny himself, take up his cross, and follow Me. For whoever wants to save his
life will lose it, but whoever loses his life
because of Me will find it. What will it
benefit a man if he gains the whole world
yet loses his life? Or what will a man give
in exchange for his life? For the Son of
Man is going to come with His angels in
the glory of His Father, and then He will

reward each according to what he has done. ~ Matthew 16:24–27

God's Manual

For whatever was written in the past was written for our instruction, so that we may have hope through endurance and through the encouragement from the Scriptures. ~ Romans 15:4

Receive Instruction

But as for you, continue in what you have learned and firmly believed. You know those who taught you, and you know that from childhood you have known the sacred Scriptures, which are able to give you wisdom for salvation through faith in Christ Jesus. ~ 2 Timothy 3:14–15

Inspired Words

All Scripture is inspired by God and is profitable for teaching, for rebuking, for correcting, for training in righteousness, so that the man of God may be complete, equipped for every good work.
~ 2 Timothy 3:16–17

The Instruction of the Lord

The instruction of the LORD is perfect,
renewing one's life; the testimony of the
LORD is trustworthy, making the inexpe-
rienced wise.

The precepts of the LORD are right,
making the heart glad; the command
of the LORD is radiant, making the eyes
light up.

The fear of the LORD is pure, endur-
ing forever; the ordinances of the LORD
are reliable and altogether righteous.

They are more desirable than gold—
than an abundance of pure gold; and
sweeter than honey, which comes from
the honeycomb.

In addition, Your servant is warned
by them; there is great reward in keeping
them. ~ Psalm 19:7–11

The Choice to Obey

I am resolved to obey Your statutes
to the very end. ~ Psalm 119:112

Quotes to Encourage You

Every time you make a choice you are turning the central part of you, the part that chooses, into something a little different from what it was before. ~ C. S. Lewis

In any moment of decision the best thing you can do is the right thing, the next best thing is the wrong thing, and the worst thing you can do is nothing. ~ Theodore Roosevelt

Between two evils, choose neither. Between two goods, choose both. ~ T. Edwards

Our capacity to choose changes constantly with our practice of life. The longer we continue to make the wrong decisions, the more our hearts harden; the more often we make the right decisions, the more our hearts soften or better, perhaps, come alive. ~ Eric Fromm

The decision we all face is this: whether to consciously lock God out of our lives or open the door of our heart and invite Jesus Christ to come in. ~ Luis Palau

Thus we see that the all important thing is not killing or giving life, drinking or not drinking, living in the town or the country, being lucky or unlucky, winning or losing. It is how we win, how we lose, how we live or die, finally, how we choose. ~ R. H. Blyth

Good and evil both increase at compound interest. That is why the little decisions you and I make every day are of such infinite importance. ~ C. S. Lewis

God never gives us discernment in order that we may criticize, but that we may intercede.
~ Oswald Chambers

God has no pleasure in afflicting us, but He will not keep back even the most painful chastisement if He can but thereby guide His beloved child to come home and abide in the beloved Son. ~ Andrew Murray

It hurts when God has to PRY things out of our hand!
~ Corrie Ten Boom

Prayer

Lord, be with me as I make choices that make a difference in my life. Guard my heart and my mind, protecting me from those things that I cannot know as a new decision must be made. Help me to stay close to You and to Your Word so that I may know without doubt the best choices to make. Keep my heart ever soft and pliable, willing to be shaped and molded by Your gracious hand. Amen.

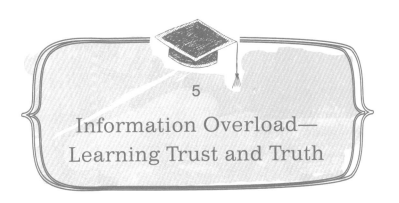

5

Information Overload—
Learning Trust and Truth

*In God alone there is faithfulness and faith in the trust that
we may hold to him, to his promise and to his guidance. To
hold to God is to rely on the fact that God is there for me,
and to live in this certainty. ~ Karl Barth*

One aspect of graduation is that it takes you from a
place of certainty, knowing what you are doing each day
as you prepare for classes or tests, and then releases you
from all you've known. It causes you to have to step out
beyond the familiar and into arenas that are brand new.
It's a good thing of course, but it requires discernment.
It means that you have to learn to trust yourself and to
trust God and to seek the truth. In a world of informa-
tion overload, this is not always an easy proposition.

The steadfast and unchanging nature of God is comforting because once you've learned to trust Him, you know you can always trust Him. He isn't fickle. He doesn't say anything He doesn't mean. He's there for you! You can rely on Him and hold on to His promises for you because nothing on earth can separate you from Him and His love. Nothing that happens in the news, or at a job, or in your family, can take this truth from you. But you must be the one who holds on, who leans in, and trusts God for your present circumstances and your future.

So go ahead, and let the noise of the world fade away as you look with a trusting heart to God for all that you need.

Scripture to Guide You

The Truth Sets You Free

> As He was saying these things, many believed in Him. So Jesus said to the Jews who had believed Him, "If you continue in My word, you really are My disciples. You will know the truth, and the truth will set you free." ~ John 8:30–32

Your Word Is Truth

The entirety of Your word is truth, and all Your righteous judgments endure forever. ~ Psalm 119:160

Blessings and Actions

But be doers of the word and not hearers only, deceiving yourselves. Because if anyone is a hearer of the word and not a doer, he is like a man looking at his own face in a mirror. For he looks at himself, goes away, and immediately forgets what kind of man he was. But the one who looks intently into the perfect law of freedom and perseveres in it, and is not a forgetful hearer but one who does good works—this person will be blessed in what he does. ~ James 1:22–25

Standing for Truth

For we are not able to do anything against the truth, but only for the truth. ~ 2 Corinthians 13:8

Speaking the Truth

Then we will no longer be little children, tossed by the waves and blown around by every wind of teaching, by human cunning with cleverness in the techniques of deceit. But speaking the truth in love, let us grow in every way into Him who is the head—Christ. ~ Ephesians 4:14–15

What Can You Believe?

Dear friends, do not believe every spirit, but test the spirits to determine if they are from God, because many false prophets have gone out into the world.

This is how you know the Spirit of God: Every spirit who confesses that Jesus Christ has come in the flesh is from God. But every spirit who does not confess Jesus is not from God. This is the spirit of the antichrist; you have heard that he is coming, and he is already in the world now. ~ 1 John 4:1–3

Keep a Clear Head

For the time will come when they will not tolerate sound doctrine, but according to their own desires, will multiply teachers for themselves because they have an itch to hear something new. They will turn away from hearing the truth and will turn aside to myths. But as for you, be serious about everything, endure hardship, do the work of an evangelist, fulfill your ministry. ~ 2 Timothy 4:3–5

The Spirit of Truth

When the Spirit of truth comes, He will guide you into all the truth. For He will not speak on His own, but He will speak whatever He hears. He will also declare to you what is to come. ~ John 16:13

God Is My Rock

The LORD is my rock, my fortress, and my deliverer, my God, my mountain where I seek refuge, my shield and the horn of my salvation, my stronghold. ~ Psalm 18:2

Hope in the Lord

The man who trusts in the LORD, whose
confidence indeed is the LORD, is blessed.
~ Jeremiah 17:7

I Am the Truth

Jesus told him, "I am the way, the truth,
and the life. No one comes to the Father
except through Me." ~ John 14:6

God's Word Is Truth

Sanctify them by the truth; Your word is
truth. ~ John 17:17

Ponder These Truths

Finally brothers, whatever is true, whatever is honorable, whatever is just, whatever is pure, whatever is lovely, whatever
is commendable—if there is any moral
excellence and if there is any praise—
dwell on these things. ~ Philippians 4:8

Walk in Truth

> I have no greater joy than this: to hear
> that my children are walking in the truth.
> ~ 3 John 4

Quotes to Encourage You

*All human discoveries seem to be made only for the
purpose of confirming more and more strongly the
truths contained in the sacred Scriptures.*
~ John Herschel

*I know God won't give me anything I can't handle. I
just wish he didn't trust me so much. ~ Mother Teresa*

Quiet minds that rest in God cannot be perplexed or frightened, but go on in fortune or misfortune at their private pace, like a clock during a thunderstorm.
~ Robert Louis Stevenson

Oh, how great peace and quietness would he possess who should cut off all vain anxiety and place all his confidence in God. ~ Thomas à Kempis

Trust in yourself and you are doomed to disappointment. Trust in your friends and they will die and leave you. Trust in money and you may have it taken away from you. Trust in reputation and some slanderous tongues will blast it. But trust in God and you are never to be confounded in time or in eternity.
~ Dwight Moody

Set all your trust in God and fear not the language of the world; for the more despite, shame, and reproof that you receive from the world, the more is your merit in the sight of God. ~ Julian of Norwich

Truth does not change because it is or is not believed by a majority of the people. ~ Giordano Bruno

Truth is the foundation of all knowledge and the cement of all societies. ~ John Dryden

All I have seen teaches me to trust the Creator for all I have not seen. ~ Emerson

Prayer

Dear Lord, quiet the noise of the world so that I may hear Your truth. Help me to trust in Your voice and to listen for it every place I go. Help me to build on Your foundation of truth and trust so that I can carry on any work I may do to Your glory. Grant me discernment in the people I choose to be around, in the places I choose to go, and in the work I do so that I may stand firm in my faith and my life direction. Amen.

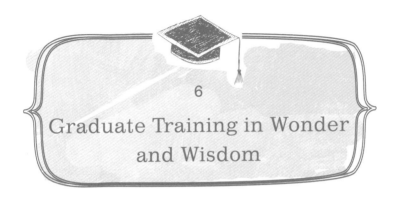

6

Graduate Training in Wonder and Wisdom

The word of God will stand a thousand readings;
and he who has gone over it most frequently is the surest of
finding new wonders there. ~ James Hamilton

As a recent graduate, you're used to hitting the books. You know a lot about what it means to burn the midnight oil so that you're prepared for the next class or test.

The biggest selling book of all time is the Bible and though you may already be a Bible reader, you might find it inspiring to be more of a Bible student. As a student, you begin to look for the meaning in the passages you read or in the stories that serve as examples for living a good life. More than that, you might open your mind and your heart to its wisdom, seeking the wonders of timeless truths and possibilities.

You're always going to be in training here on planet Earth. You're always going to be a student of life and of God's Word. Search with fresh eyes, with anticipation of finding gems of truth that you can carry with you forever.

You have been equipped by your education to do something unique and special in the world. God wants you to burn a little midnight oil with Him so that He can also equip you for the unique role that only you have in the work for His kingdom. You are His child, His beloved. He is a master teacher and is ready to help you learn more about Him at any given moment.

Wisdom and wonder awaits you!

Scripture to Guide You

First Things First

> But seek first the kingdom of God and
> His righteousness, and all these things
> will be provided for you. ~ Matthew 6:33

Turn Back to God

> Then Eliphaz the Temanite replied:
> Can a man be of any use to God?

Can even a wise man be of use to Him?

Does it delight the Almighty if you are righteous?

Does He profit if you perfect your behavior?

Does He correct you and take you to court because of your piety?

Isn't your wickedness abundant and aren't your iniquities endless?

For you took collateral from your brothers without cause, stripping off their clothes and leaving them naked.

You gave no water to the thirsty and withheld food from the famished, while the land belonged to a powerful man and an influential man lived on it.

You sent widows away empty-handed, and the strength of the fatherless was crushed.

Therefore snares surround you, and sudden dread terrifies you, or darkness, so you cannot see, and a flood of water covers you.

Isn't God as high as the heavens?

And look at the highest stars—how lofty they are!

Yet you say: "What does God know?

Can He judge through thick darkness? Clouds veil Him so that He cannot see, as He walks on the circle of the sky."

Will you continue on the ancient path that wicked men have walked?

They were snatched away before their time, and their foundations were washed away by a river.

They were the ones who said to God, "Leave us alone!" and "What can the Almighty do to us?"

But it was He who filled their houses with good things.

The counsel of the wicked is far from me!

The righteous see this and rejoice; the innocent mock them, saying, "Surely our opponents are destroyed, and fire has consumed what they left behind."

Come to terms with God and be at peace; in this way good will come to you.

Receive instruction from His mouth, and place His sayings in your heart.

If you return to the Almighty, you will be renewed.

If you banish injustice from your tent and consign your gold to the dust, the gold of Ophir to the stones in the wadis, the Almighty will be your gold and your finest silver.

Then you will delight in the Almighty and lift up your face to God.

You will pray to Him, and He will hear you, and you will fulfill your vows.

When you make a decision, it will be carried out, and light will shine on your ways.

When others are humiliated and you say, "Lift them up," God will save the humble.

He will even rescue the guilty one, who will be rescued by the purity of your hands. ~ Job 22

Job's Reply to Eliphaz

Then Job answered:

Today also my complaint is bitter.

His hand is heavy despite my groaning.

If only I knew how to find Him, so that I could go to His throne.

I would plead my case before Him and fill my mouth with arguments.

I would learn how He would answer me; and understand what He would say to me.

Would He prosecute me forcefully?

No, He will certainly pay attention to me.

Then an upright man could reason with Him, and I would escape from my Judge forever.

If I go east, He is not there, and if I go west, I cannot perceive Him.

When He is at work to the north, I cannot see Him; when He turns south, I cannot find Him.

Yet He knows the way I have taken; when He has tested me, I will emerge as pure gold.

My feet have followed in His tracks; I have kept to His way and not turned aside.

I have not departed from the commands of His lips; I have treasured the words of His mouth more than my daily food.

But He is unchangeable; who can oppose Him?

He does what He desires.

He will certainly accomplish what He has decreed for me, and He has many more things like these in mind.

Therefore I am terrified in His presence; when I consider this, I am afraid of Him.

God has made my heart faint; the Almighty has terrified me.

Yet I am not destroyed by the darkness, by the thick darkness that covers my face.

Why does the Almighty not reserve times for judgment?

Why do those who know Him never see His days?

The wicked displace boundary markers.

They steal a flock and provide pasture for it.

They drive away the donkeys owned by the fatherless and take the widow's ox as collateral.

They push the needy off the road; the poor of the land are forced into hiding.

Like wild donkeys in the desert, the poor go out to their task of foraging for food; the wilderness provides nourishment for their children.

They gather their fodder in the field and glean the vineyards of the wicked.

Without clothing, they spend the night naked, having no covering against the cold.

Drenched by mountain rains, they huddle against the rocks, shelterless.

The fatherless infant is snatched from the breast; the nursing child of the poor is seized as collateral.

Without clothing, they wander about naked.

They carry sheaves but go hungry.

They crush olives in their presses; they tread the winepresses, but go thirsty.

From the city, men groan; the mortally wounded cry for help, yet God pays no attention to this crime.

The wicked are those who rebel against the light.

They do not recognize its ways or stay on its paths.

The murderer rises at dawn to kill
the poor and needy, and by night he
becomes a thief.

The adulterer's eye watches for
twilight, thinking: No eye will see me; he
covers his face.

In the dark they break into houses;
by day they lock themselves in, never
experiencing the light.

For the morning is like darkness to
them.

Surely they are familiar with the terrors of darkness!

They float on the surface of the water.

Their section of the land is cursed, so
that they never go to their vineyards.

As dry ground and heat snatch away
the melted snow, so Sheol steals those
who have sinned.

The womb forgets them; worms feed
on them; they are remembered no more.

So injustice is broken like a tree.

They prey on the childless woman
who is unable to conceive, and do not
deal kindly with the widow.

Yet God drags away the mighty by His power; when He rises up, they have no assurance of life.

He gives them a sense of security, so they can rely on it, but His eyes watch over their ways.

They are exalted for a moment, then they are gone; they are brought low and shrivel up like everything else.

They wither like heads of grain.

If this is not true, then who can prove me a liar and show that my speech is worthless? ~ Job 23–24

Bildad Speaks

Then Bildad the Shuhite replied:

Dominion and dread belong to Him, the One who establishes harmony in the heavens.

Can His troops be numbered?

Does His light not shine on everyone?

How can a person be justified before God?

How can one born of woman be pure?

If even the moon does not shine and the stars are not pure in His sight, how much less man, who is a maggot, and the son of man, who is a worm! ~ Job 25

Job's Reply to Bildad

Then Job answered:

How you have helped the powerless and delivered the arm that is weak!

How you have counseled the unwise and thoroughly explained the path to success!

Who did you speak these words to?

Whose breath came out of your mouth?

The departed spirits tremble beneath the waters and all that inhabit them.

Sheol is naked before God, and Abaddon has no covering.

He stretches the northern skies over empty space; He hangs the earth on nothing.

He wraps up the waters in His clouds, yet the clouds do not burst beneath their weight.

He obscures the view of His throne, spreading His cloud over it.

He laid out the horizon on the surface of the waters at the boundary between light and darkness.

The pillars that hold up the sky tremble, astounded at His rebuke.

By His power He stirred the sea, and by His understanding He crushed Rahab.

By His breath the heavens gained their beauty; His hand pierced the fleeing serpent.

These are but the fringes of His ways; how faint is the word we hear of Him!

Who can understand His mighty thunder?

Job continued his discourse, saying:

As God lives, who has deprived me of justice, and the Almighty who has made me bitter, as long as my breath is still in me and the breath from God remains in my nostrils, my lips will not speak unjustly, and my tongue will not utter deceit.

I will never affirm that you are right.

I will maintain my integrity until I die.

I will cling to my righteousness and never let it go.

My conscience will not accuse me as long as I live!

May my enemy be like the wicked and my opponent like the unjust.

For what hope does the godless man have when he is cut off, when God takes away his life?

Will God hear his cry when distress comes on him?

Will he delight in the Almighty?

Will he call on God at all times?

I will teach you about God's power.

I will not conceal what the Almighty has planned.

All of you have seen this for yourselves, why do you keep up this empty talk?

This is a wicked man's lot from God, the inheritance the ruthless receive from the Almighty.

Even if his children increase, they are destined for the sword;his descendants will never have enough food.

Those who survive him will be buried by the plague, yet their widows will not weep for them.

Though he piles up silver like dust and heaps up a wardrobe like clay—he may heap it up, but the righteous will wear it, and the innocent will divide up his silver.

The house he built is like a moth's cocoon or a booth set up by a watchman.

He lies down wealthy, but will do so no more; when he opens his eyes, it is gone.

Terrors overtake him like a flood; a storm wind sweeps him away at night.

An east wind picks him up, and he is gone; it carries him away from his place.

It blasts at him without mercy, while he flees desperately from its grasp.

It claps its hands at him and scorns him from its place. ~ Job 26–27

Job's Hymn to Wisdom

Surely there is a mine for silver and a place where gold is refined.

Iron is taken from the ground, and copper is smelted from ore.

A miner puts an end to the darkness; he probes the deepest recesses for ore in the gloomy darkness.

He cuts a shaft far from human habitation, in places unknown to those who walk above ground.

Suspended far away from people, the miners swing back and forth.

Food may come from the earth, but below the surface the earth is transformed as by fire.

Its rocks are a source of sapphire, containing flecks of gold.

No bird of prey knows that path; no falcon's eye has seen it.

Proud beasts have never walked on it; no lion has ever prowled over it.

The miner strikes the flint and transforms the mountains at their foundations.

He cuts out channels in the rocks, and his eyes spot every treasure.

He dams up the streams from flowing so that he may bring to light what is hidden.

But where can wisdom be found, and where is understanding located?

No man can know its value, since it cannot be found in the land of the living.

The ocean depths say, "It's not in me," while the sea declares, "I don't have it."

Gold cannot be exchanged for it, and silver cannot be weighed out for its price.

Wisdom cannot be valued in the gold of Ophir, in precious onyx or sapphire.

Gold and glass do not compare with it, and articles of fine gold cannot be exchanged for it.

Coral and quartz are not worth mentioning.

The price of wisdom is beyond pearls.

Topaz from Cush cannot compare with it, and it cannot be valued in pure gold.

Where then does wisdom come from, and where is understanding located?

It is hidden from the eyes of every living thing and concealed from the birds of the sky.

Abaddon and Death say, "We have heard news of it with our ears."

But God understands the way to wisdom, and He knows its location.

For He looks to the ends of the earth and sees everything under the heavens.

When God fixed the weight of the wind and limited the water by measure, when He established a limit for the rain and a path for the lightning, He considered wisdom and evaluated it; He established it and examined it.

He said to mankind, "The fear of the Lord is this: wisdom. And to turn from evil is understanding." ~ Job 28

Growing Up in Faith

Then we will no longer be little children, tossed by the waves and blown around by every wind of teaching, by human cunning with cleverness in the techniques of deceit. But speaking the truth in love, let us grow in every way into Him who is the head—Christ. ~ Ephesians 4:14–15

Study in Delight

The Lord's works are great, studied by all who delight in them. All that He does is splendid and majestic; His righteousness endures forever. ~ Psalm 111:2–3

God Can Do Anything

Should anyone try to speak with you when you are exhausted? Yet who can keep from speaking?

Indeed, you have instructed many and have strengthened weak hands.

Your words have steadied the one who was stumbling and braced the knees that were buckling.

But now that this has happened to you, you have become exhausted. It strikes you, and you are dismayed.
~ Job 4:2–5

Humble Yourself

In the same way, you younger men, be subject to the elders. And all of you clothe yourselves with humility toward one another, because God resists the proud but gives grace to the humble. Humble yourselves, therefore, under the mighty hand of God, so that He may exalt you at the proper time, casting all your care on Him, because He cares about you. ~ 1 Peter 5:5–7

Seek Wisdom

My son, if you accept my words and store up my commands within you, listening closely to wisdom and directing your heart to understanding; furthermore, if you call out to insight and lift your voice to understanding, if you seek it like silver and search for it like hidden treasure, then you will understand the fear of the LORD and discover the knowledge of God. For the LORD gives wisdom; from His mouth come knowledge and understanding. He stores up success for the upright; He is a shield for those who live with integrity so that He may guard the paths of justice and protect the way of His loyal followers. Then you will understand righteousness, justice, and integrity—every good path. For wisdom will enter your mind, and knowledge will delight your heart. Discretion will watch over you, and understanding will guard you, rescuing you from the way of evil— from the one who says perverse things.
~ Proverbs 2:1–12

Ask God for Wisdom

Now if any of you lacks wisdom, he should ask God, who gives to all generously and without criticizing, and it will be given to him. But let him ask in faith without doubting. For the doubter is like the surging sea, driven and tossed by the wind. That person should not expect to receive anything from the Lord.
~ James 1:5–7

God Gives You the Words

For I will give you such words and a wisdom that none of your adversaries will be able to resist or contradict. ~ Luke 21:15

The Beginning of Wisdom

The fear of the Lord is the beginning of wisdom; all who follow His instructions have good insight. His praise endures forever. ~ Psalm 111:10

Wisdom's Instructions

The fear of the Lord is what wisdom teaches, and humility comes before honor. ~ Proverbs 15:33

God Gives Wisdom

This also comes from the LORD of Hosts. He gives wonderful advice; He gives great wisdom. ~ Isaiah 28:29

The Sun Stood Still

And the sun stood still and the moon stopped until the nation took vengeance on its enemies.

Isn't this written in the Book of Jashar?

So the sun stopped in the middle of the sky and delayed its setting almost a full day. ~ Joshua 10:13

Beyond Imagination

But as it is written: "What eye did not see and ear did not hear, and what never entered the human mind—God prepared this for those who love Him."
~ 1 Corinthians 2:9

Apply Your Heart to Wisdom

Teach us to number our days carefully so that we may develop wisdom in our hearts. ~ Psalm 90:12

Get Wisdom

Wisdom is supreme—so get wisdom.
And whatever else you get, get understanding. ~ Proverbs 4:7

Quotes to Encourage You

*If you picture the Bible to be a mighty tree and every
word a little branch, I have shaken every one of those
branches because I wanted to know what it was and
what it meant. ~ Martin Luther*

*The word of God will stand a thousand readings; and
he who has gone over it most frequently is the surest of
finding new wonders there. ~ James Hamilton*

Read the Bible as though it were something entirely unfamiliar, as though it had not been set before you ready-made. Face the book with a new attitude as something new. ~ Martin Buber

Apply yourself wholly to the Scriptures, and apply the Scriptures wholly to yourself. ~ Bengel

When you read God's word, you must constantly be saying to yourself, "It's talking to me and it's about me." ~ Kierkegaard

Some read the Bible to learn and some read the Bible to hear from heaven. ~ Andrew Murray

The more you read the Bible, and the more you meditate upon it, the more you will be astonished by it.
~ C. H. Spurgeon

When you read the Bible, you will know it is the word of God, because you will have found it the key to your own heart, your own happiness and your duty.
~ Woodrow Wilson

Thorough knowledge of the Bible is worth more than a college education. ~ Theodore Roosevelt

Knowledge is the power of the mind. Wisdom is the power of the soul. ~ Julie Shannahan

Knowledge comes, but wisdom lingers.
~ Alfred Tennyson

If our children have the background of a godly, happy
home and this unshakable faith that the Bible is indeed
the Word of God, they will have a foundation that the
forces of hell cannot shake. ~ Ruth Graham

What the church lacks in our day is not a reliable text
of the bible, but the fiath in the sufficiently reliable
text. ~ John Piper

Prayer

Lord, be with me when I study Your Word. Quiet my mind and my spirit so that I might soak up the gems of wisdom You have for me. Help me to look with fresh eyes and an eager heart to seek more of You. Bless my efforts through Your Holy Spirit to know more of You and to apply your kindness and mercy and instruction to my life. Amen.

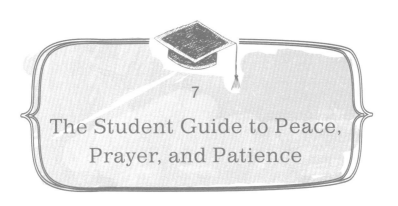

7

The Student Guide to Peace, Prayer, and Patience

What can be more excellent than prayer; what is more profitable to our life; what sweeter to our souls; what more sublime, in the course of our whole life, than the practice of prayer! ~ Augustine of Hippo

Approaches to prayer are probably as varied as the people praying. How-to manuals abound, but the truth is, God isn't as much concerned about your approach as in the fact that you do approach. He invites you to come anytime, anywhere you are, just as you are. You don't need to have had a course in Prayer 101 or have a Ph.D. in praying before God will acknowledge you.

The good news gets even better because He always holds the line open for you. He awaits your call and picks up on the first ring tone. You call, He's there! It's that simple!

Yet somehow, we've made prayer into some kind of mystery. We wonder if we're allowed to pray about everything or just certain things. We wonder if God really hears us and if He does if He'll really answer us. We wonder because we haven't been praying enough and often enough to actually know how prayer works.

If you're curious, and since you've been a student for some time, you're probably curious about things, then be curious about prayer. Experiment with your own approach, your own style, the time of day that works best for you, and the moments when you feel like God answered. The more you develop a prayer practice, the quicker you'll sense your connection to God.

Prayer takes practice and patience. But like other things of God, the more you embrace your prayerful heart, the more peace you'll have in your life. If you know how to talk, you know how to pray.

Scripture to Guide You

Thinking of You

> When I think of You as I lie on my bed,
> I meditate on You during the night
> watches because You are my helper; I
> will rejoice in the shadow of Your wings.

I follow close to You; Your right hand holds on to me. ~ Psalm 63:6–8

Let Me Experience You

Let me experience Your faithful love in the morning, for I trust in You. Reveal to me the way I should go because I long for You. Rescue me from my enemies, LORD; I come to You for protection. Teach me to do Your will, for You are my God. May Your gracious Spirit lead me on level ground. ~ Psalm 143:8–10

Pray About Everything

Don't worry about anything, but in everything, through prayer and petition with thanksgiving, let your requests be made known to God. And the peace of God, which surpasses every thought, will guard your hearts and minds in Christ Jesus. ~ Philippians 4:6–7

Pray with Confidence

Now this is the confidence we have before Him: Whenever we ask anything according to His will, He hears us. And if we know that He hears whatever we ask, we know that we have what we have asked Him for. ~ 1 John 5:14–15

Don't Give Up!

"Keep asking, and it will be given to you. Keep searching, and you will find. Keep knocking, and the door will be opened to you. For everyone who asks receives, and the one who searches finds, and to the one who knocks, the door will be opened." ~ Matthew 7:7–8

Approaching the Throne

Therefore, since we have a great high priest who has passed through the heavens—Jesus the Son of God—let us hold fast to the confession. For we do not have a high priest who is unable to sympathize with our weaknesses, but One who has been tested in every way as we are, yet without sin. Therefore let us approach the throne of grace with bold-ness, so that we may receive mercy and find grace to help us at the proper time. ~ Hebrews 4:14–16

Accept My Prayers

May the words of my mouth and the meditation of my heart be acceptable to You, Lord, my rock and my Redeemer. ~ Psalm 19:14

Seek the Lord

Seek the Lord while He may be found; call to Him while He is near. ~ Isaiah 55:6

God Knows Your Needs

Don't be like them, because your Father knows the things you need before you ask Him. ~ Matthew 6:8

The Lord's Prayer

"Therefore, you should pray like this: Our Father in heaven, Your name be honored as holy. Your kingdom come. Your will be done on earth as it is in heaven." ~ Matthew 6:9–10

Two or Three

"For where two or three are gathered together in My name, I am there among them." ~ Matthew 18:20

Prayer and Forgiveness

And whenever you stand praying, if you have anything against anyone, forgive him, so that your Father in heaven will also forgive you your wrongdoing. ~ Mark 11:25

Ask in Jesus' Name

"Whatever you ask in My name, I will do it so that the Father may be glorified in the Son." ~ John 14:13

Don't Stop Praying

Pray constantly. ~ 1 Thessalonians 5:17

Pray for Each Other

Therefore, confess your sins to one another and pray for one another, so that you may be healed. The urgent request

of a righteous person is very powerful in
its effect. ~ James 5:16

The Lord Hears Your Prayers

Because the eyes of the Lord are on
the righteous and His ears are open to
their request. But the face of the Lord is
against those who do what is evil.
~ 1 Peter 3:12

Quotes to Encourage You

*If you are swept off your feet, it's time
to get on your knees. ~ Fred Beck*

*In the morning, prayer is the key that opens to us the
treasures of God's mercies and blessings; in the evening,
it is the key that shuts us up under His protection and
safeguard. ~ Henry Ward Beecher*

Prayer is not learned in the classroom, but in the closet.
~ E. M. Bounds

In prayer, it is better to have a heart without words,
than words without a heart. ~ John Bunyan

Heaven is full of answers to prayers for which no one
ever bothered to ask. ~ Billy Graham

Pray as if everything depended on God, and act as if
everything depended on you. ~ Ignatius of Loyola

None can believe how powerful prayer is, and what it is able to effect, but those who have learned it by experience. ~ Martin Luther

One may study because the brain is hungry for knowledge, even Bible knowledge. But one prays because the soul is hungry for God. ~ Leonard Ravenhill (adapted)

Love to pray. Feel often during the day the need for prayer, and take trouble to pray. Prayer enlarges the heart until it is capable of containing God's gift of Himself. Ask and seek and your heart will grow big enough to receive Him. ~ Mother Teresa

Prayer is love in need appealing to love in power. ~ Robert Moffatt

Prayer is not a substitute for work, thinking watching, suffering, or giving; prayer is a support for all other efforts. ~ George Butyric

Prayer

Dear Lord, thank You for being there. Thank You for hearing my prayers and for listening closely to my heart. When I don't know what to say or how to pray, thank You for giving me a sense of peace. When I have great concerns for others, thank You for receiving my requests. In all ways and for always, I thank You for your guidance and love. Amen.

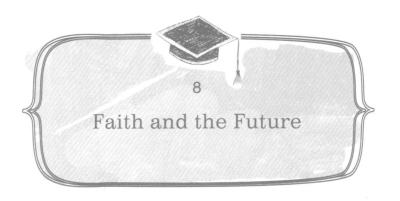

8

Faith and the Future

It has been well said that no one ever sank under
the burden of the day. It is when tomorrow's burden
is added to the burden of today that the weight is more
than a person can bear. Never load yourselves so, my friends.
If you find yourselves so loaded, at least remember this:
it is your own doing, not God's. He begs you to leave the
future to Him and mind the present. ~ George MacDonald

As a recent graduate, you can't help being over-whelmed with hopes and fears about the future. You have to make many new choices, try things you've never tried before and go after dreams that may seem at best like shining apples on the highest branch of a tree many miles away.

Sure, you're aware that you have to take one day at a time and go step by step, but still you may hold the future up as the place of possibility. The fact is that all your possibility is resting in today. Today is the space God has given you to work things through. Today is the day where you can embrace a future with faith or with a sense that everything depends on you. How will you choose?

If your choice is to walk in faith, pray, and surrender your life to God and when you start each day with that idea, your future will unfold according to God's grace and mercy. By now, you have enough life experience to recognize surrender can feel difficult.

Most of us hope that God will give us a flashlight so that we can see what is coming around the bend as we walk along. We hope that somehow we'll discover the path for ourselves. The same God who put a pillar of fire in the night sky to guide the Israelites as they walked to a Promised Land, is the One who guides you as well. Every time you surrender to Him, a Light comes on. Your future then is assured. Have faith in all He has designed for you!

Scripture to Guide You

Happy in the Lord

> How happy is everyone who fears the
> LORD, who walks in His ways! You will

surely eat what your hands have worked
for. You will be happy, and it will go well
for you. ~ Psalm 128:1–2

Don't Give Up!

Therefore we do not give up. Even
though our outer person is being
destroyed, our inner person is being
renewed day by day. For our momentary
light affliction is producing for us an
absolutely incomparable eternal weight
of glory. So we do not focus on what is
seen, but on what is unseen. For what is
seen is temporary, but what is unseen is
eternal. ~ 2 Corinthians 4:16–18

God Is Our Help

God is our refuge and strength, a helper
who is always found in times of trouble.
Therefore we will not be afraid, though
the earth trembles and the mountains
topple into the depths of the seas.
~ Psalm 46:1–2

The Eyes of Faith

Therefore, since we also have such a
large cloud of witnesses surrounding us,
let us lay aside every weight and the sin
that so easily ensnares us. Let us run with
endurance the race that lies before us,
keeping our eyes on Jesus, the source and
perfecter of our faith, who for the joy
that lay before Him endured a cross and
despised the shame and has sat down at
the right hand of God's throne.
~ Hebrews 12:1–2

God's Promise

So don't throw away your confidence,
which has a great reward. For you need
endurance, so that after you have done
God's will, you may receive what was
promised.

For yet in a very little while, the
Coming One will come and not delay.
~ Hebrews 10:35–37

Trust in the Lord

Trust in the LORD and do what is good;
dwell in the land and live securely. Take

delight in the LORD, and He will give
you your heart's desires.

Commit your way to the LORD; trust
in Him, and He will act, making your
righteousness shine like the dawn, your
justice like the noonday.

Be silent before the LORD and wait
expectantly for Him; do not be agitated
by one who prospers in his way, by the
man who carries out evil plans. ~ Psalm
37:3–7

I have been young and now I am old, yet
I have not seen the righteous abandoned
or his children begging for bread. He is
always generous, always lending,
and his children are a blessing. ~ Psalm
37:25–26

The Lord Is My Shepherd

The LORD is my shepherd; there is
nothing I lack. He lets me lie down in
green pastures; He leads me beside quiet
waters. He renews my life; He leads me
along the right paths for His name's sake.
Even when I go through the darkest val-
ley, I fear no danger, for You are with me;

Your rod and Your staff—they comfort me. You prepare a table before me in the presence of my enemies; You anoint my head with oil; my cup overflows. Only goodness and faithful love will pursue me all the days of my life, and I will dwell in the house of the LORD as long as I live.
~ Psalm 23

Walking With the Lord

For this reason also, since the day we heard this, we haven't stopped praying for you. We are asking that you may be filled with the knowledge of His will in all wisdom and spiritual understanding, so that you may walk worthy of the Lord, fully pleasing to Him, bearing fruit in every good work and growing in the knowledge of God. May you be strengthened with all power, according to His glorious might, for all endurance and patience, with joy giving thanks to the Father, who has enabled you to share in the saints' inheritance in the light.
~ Colossians 1:9–12

Don't Worry

"This is why I tell you: Don't worry about your life, what you will eat or what you will drink; or about your body, what you will wear. Isn't life more than food and the body more than clothing? Look at the birds of the sky: They don't sow or reap or gather into barns, yet your heavenly Father feeds them. Aren't you worth more than they? Can any of you add a single cubit to his height by worrying? And why do you worry about clothes? Learn how the wildflowers of the field grow: they don't labor or spin thread. Yet I tell you that not even Solomon in all his splendor was adorned like one of these! If that's how God clothes the grass of the field, which is here today and thrown into the furnace tomorrow, won't He do much more for you—you of little faith?" ~ Matthew 6:25–30

Don't Worry About Tomorrow

Therefore don't worry about tomorrow, because tomorrow will worry about itself. Each day has enough trouble of its own. ~ Matthew 6:34

Getting Out of Darkness

If I say, "Surely the darkness will hide me, and the light around me will be night"—even the darkness is not dark to You. The night shines like the day; darkness and light are alike to You. ~ Psalm 139:11–12

Assurance of Faith

Let us draw near with a true heart in full assurance of faith, our hearts sprinkled clean from an evil conscience and our bodies washed in pure water. Let us hold on to the confession of our hope without wavering, for He who promised is faithful. ~ Hebrews 10:22–23

God Works for Your Good

We know that all things work together for the good of those who love God: those who are called according to His purpose. ~ Romans 8:28

Quotes to Encourage You

God is continually drawing us to Himself in everything we experience. ~ Gerard Hughes

What were we made for? To know God.
What aim should we have in life? To know God.
What is the eternal life that Jesus gives! To know God.
What is the best thing in life? To know God.
What in humans gives God most pleasure? Knowledge of himself. ~ J. I. Packer

Never mistake knowledge for wisdom.
One helps you make a living. The other helps you make a life. ~ Sandra Carey

When I was young I was sure of everything; in a few years, having been mistaken a thousand times, I was not half so sure of most things as I was before; at present, I am hardly sure of anything but what God has revealed to me. ~ John Wesley

Trust the past to God's mercy, the present to God's love, and the future to God's providence. ~ Augustine of Hippo

It is because of faith that we exchange the present for the future. ~ Sigmaringen

Regret looks back.
Worry looks around.
Faith looks up. ~ John Mason

Do not worry or fret that God has given more faith to others than He has given to you. Rest assured in the fact that God has imparted enough faith to you to make sure you are covered from head to toe. ~ Rick Renner

When you get to the end of all the light you know and it's time to step into the darkness and the unknown, faith is knowing that one of two things will happen: either you will be given something solid to stand on, or you will be taught how to fly. ~ Edward Teller

The great thing is to be found at one's post as a child of God, living each day as though it were our last, but planning as though our world might last a hundred years. ~ C. S. Lewis

Prayer

Lord, thank You for all You've taught me so far. Thank You for guiding my work when I was a student, and for allowing me to be Your student for the rest of my life. Teach me those things that will help me to be wise. Walk with me as I seek the paths to the future and make plans for the things I'll do. Protect my spirit and my heart as I seek to know more of You and what it means to live in the present moment by Your grace. Thank You for shining Your great light on me. Amen.

9

New Goals, New Direction, New You!

The rational questions:
1. Where am I?
2. Where do I want to be?
3. How do I know I am getting there?
~ Author Unknown

The amazing part of being a graduate is the awareness that you have already achieved a significant life goal. You've already played and won a prize at the game of life and so you know you can do it. You know what it's like to stand in the winner's circle.

The difficult part of being a graduate is that you don't get to stand in that circle very long. You are expected to move on, to grow, and to set a new goal. That sounds easy enough when things fall into place nicely and the steps you need to take line up for you. But, what if they don't? What if your plans to go to college or graduate school or nursing school suddenly change because of factors you never anticipated? What if your goals are interrupted?

Sometimes you may truly find yourself in a place of wondering where you are in life. You may not even know for sure where you want to go or where you want to be. It's okay to be still for a while. It's okay to simply lean on God. He already knows your destination and He will never leave your side. Obstacles may come and temporary road blocks will certainly happen, but your life purpose will not be lost. God knows what you need and if you surrender your goals and your dreams and your plans to Him, you'll be directed and fulfilled. Your life matters to Him…it always has, and it always will! With time and with faith, you'll get where you're meant to go.

Scripture to Guide You

God Is Your Strength

> I love You, LORD, my strength. The LORD is my rock, my fortress, and my deliverer, my God, my mountain where I seek refuge, my shield and the horn of my salvation, my stronghold. ~ Psalm 18:1–2

You Have Divine Help

Your life should be free from the love of
money. Be satisfied with what you have,
for He Himself has said, I will never
leave you or forsake you. Therefore, we
may boldly say: The Lord is my helper;
I will not be afraid. What can man do to
me? ~ Hebrews 13:5–6

When You Are Uncertain

Cast your burden on the LORD, and He
will support you; He will never allow the
righteous to be shaken. ~ Psalm 55:22

Why You Can Trust God

Do you not know? Have you not heard?
Yahweh is the everlasting God, the
Creator of the whole earth. He never
grows faint or weary; there is no limit to
His understanding. He gives strength to
the weary and strengthens the powerless.
Youths may faint and grow weary, and
young men stumble and fall, but those
who trust in the Lord will renew their
strength; they will soar on wings like
eagles; they will run and not grow weary;

they will walk and not faint. ~ Isaiah
40:28–31

Why Should You Worry?

"This is why I tell you: "Don't worry
about your life, what you will eat or what
you will drink; or about your body, what
you will wear. Isn't life more than food
and the body more than clothing? Look
at the birds of the sky: they don't sow or
reap or gather into barns, yet your heavenly Father feeds them. Aren't you worth
more than they? Can any of you add a
single cubit to his height by worrying?"
~ Matthew 6:25–27

Ask for What You Need

"Keep asking, and it will be given to you.
Keep searching, and you will find. Keep
knocking, and the door will be opened
to you. For everyone who asks receives,
and the one who searches finds, and to
the one who knocks, the door will be
opened." ~ Matthew 7:7–8

Faith Moves You Forward

Jesus replied to them, "Have faith in God. I assure you: If anyone says to this mountain, 'Be lifted up and thrown into the sea,' and does not doubt in his heart, but believes that what he says will happen, it will be done for him. Therefore, I tell you, all the things you pray and ask for—believe that you have received them, and you will have them." ~ Mark 11:22–24

Remember You Have the Gift from God

Jesus answered, "If you knew the gift of God, and who is saying to you, 'Give Me a drink,' you would ask Him, and He would give you living water."

"Sir," said the woman. "You don't even have a bucket, and the well is deep. So where do you get this 'living water'? You aren't greater than our father Jacob, are you? He gave us the well and drank from it himself, as did his sons and livestock."

Jesus said, "Everyone who drinks from this water will get thirsty again. But whoever drinks from the water that I will

give him will never get thirsty again—
ever! In fact, the water I will give him
will become a well of water springing up
within him for eternal life."

"Sir," the woman said to Him, "give
me this water so I won't get thirsty and
come here to draw water."
~ John 4:10–15

Reach for God's Goal

Not that I have already reached the goal,
or am already fully mature, but I make
every effort to take hold of it because I
also have been taken hold of by Christ
Jesus. Brothers, I do not consider myself
to have taken hold of it. But one thing I
do: forgetting what is behind and reach-
ing forward to what is ahead, I pursue
as my goal the prize promised by God's
heavenly call in Christ Jesus. Therefore,
all who are mature should think this way.
And if you think differently about anything, God will reveal this to you also. In
any case, we should live up to whatever
truth we have attained. ~ Philippians
3:12–16

The Competition Is Tough

But those who want to be rich fall into temptation, a trap, and many foolish and harmful desires, which plunge people into ruin and destruction. For the love of money is a root of all kinds of evil, and by craving it, some have wandered away from the faith and pierced themselves with many pains. Now you, man of God, run from these things; but pursue righteousness, godliness, faith, love, endurance, and gentleness. Fight the good fight for the faith; take hold of eternal life, to which you were called and have made a good confession before many witnesses. ~ 1 Timothy 6:9–12

Quotes to Encourage You

If in everything you seek Jesus, you will doubtless find him. But if you seek yourself, you will indeed find yourself, to your own ruin. For you do yourself more harm by not seeking Jesus than the whole world and all your enemies could do to you. ~ Thomas à Kempis

A Look at Life from A to Z!

Avoid people and places that don't lift your spirit.
Believe in yourself.
Celebrate your efforts.
Deliver what you promise.
Enjoy the gifts God has for you today.
Forgive your past mistakes and move on.
Give more than you get.
Handle others with your heart.
Invest your time in worthwhile pursuits.
Judge all things with discernment.
Keep trying.
Love God first, then love others.
Make every minute count.
Never quit.
Open your heart and mind to good advice.
Pray.
Quit procrastinating.
Respect the rights of others.
Sleep is good for you.
Thank God for all you are right now.
Understand yourself in every possible way.
Volunteer to help others when you can.
Wait on the Lord.
eXpect great things!
Yield to wisdom.
Zero in on your goals. ~ Karen Moore

It is not enough to be good if you have the ability to be better. ~ Alberta Lee Cox

Four steps to achievement:
1. Plan purposefully.
2. Prepare prayerfully.
3. Proceed positively.
4. Purse persistently . . . and when necessary, wait patiently! ~ Adapted from William A. Ward

Procrastination and worry are the twin thieves that will try to rob you of your brilliance—but even the smallest action will drive them from your camp.
~ Gil Atkinson

You can either take action or you can hang back and hope for a miracle. Miracles are great, but they are so unpredictable. ~ Peter Drucker

A thousand words will not leave so great an impression as one deed. ~ Henrik Ibsen

It is not what life does to you that matters. It's what you do with life. ~ Karen Moore

Take a method and try it. If it fails, admit it frankly, and try another. But by all means try something. ~ F. D. Roosevelt

Many of us spend half our time wishing for things we could have if we didn't spend half our time wishing.
~ Alexander Woollcott

Do not follow where the path may lead.
Go instead where there is no path and leave a trail.
~ Ralph Waldo Emerson

Only those who attempt the absurd, achieve the impossible. ~ Author Unknown

We need to learn to set our course by the stars, not by the lights of every passing ship. ~ Omar Bradley

The possibility that we may fail in the struggle ought not to deter us from the support of a cause we believe to be just. ~ Abraham Lincoln

Do not anticipate trouble, or worry about what may never happen. Keep in the sunlight. ~ Benjamin Franklin

Prayer

Dear Lord, You are my strength and my guide. I seek Your help in all that I hope to become. I pray that You will be ever-present, ever-merciful and ever-inspiring to me as I learn to walk the path toward my dreams and my purpose. I know that I will fall down in the process and I am grateful that You will be there to pick me up and send me on my way again. Help me to remain faithful to the plan and design of my life according to Your will and purpose for me. Amen

10

You Can Do It!

When you were a little kid, you learned about life by trial and error. You learned that you could fall down, and even if you scraped your knees, you would heal in time and you could get up and try again. You learned that the world is full of boundaries, and yet it has infinite opportunities for you to explore. You witnessed the love and kindness and light of others and sometimes the dark side of others. Now that you're going into the world on your own, you'll find all these things you learned in childhood are still true, though perhaps magnified because you can't filter them through your parents' protection and guidance. You can only filter them through your own perspective and through the witness of God's Spirit within you.

The beautiful thing is that you're ready, ready to try your wings and fly on your own. You're ready to take on the world and shine your light for all to see. You're prepared for every step, and any time you don't feel prepared, you can trust that God will be at your side, gently nudging you, gently encouraging you and letting you know, "You can do it!"

The world needs the best you have to offer.

Scriptures to Guide You

God Watches Over You

> For the LORD your God has blessed you
> in all the work of your hands. He has
> watched over your journey through this
> immense wilderness. The LORD your
> God has been with you this past 40 years,
> and you have lacked nothing.
> ~ Deuteronomy 2:7

Your Work Has a Reward

> But as for you, be strong; don't be dis-
> couraged, for your work has a reward.
> ~ 2 Chronicles 15:7

The Way of Happiness

How happy is the man who does not follow the advice of the wicked, or take the path of sinners, or join a group of mockers! Instead, his delight is in the LORD's instruction, and he meditates on it day and night. ~ Psalm 1:1–2

Faith and Belief

I am certain that I will see the LORD's goodness in the land of the living. Wait for the LORD; be courageous and let your heart be strong. Wait for the LORD. ~ Psalm 27:13–14

More Life Lessons

Do not be agitated by evildoers; do not envy those who do wrong. For they wither quickly like grass and wilt like tender green plants. Trust in the LORD and do what is good; dwell in the land and live securely. Take delight in the LORD, and He will give you your heart's desires. ~ Psalm 37:1–4

Where to Place Your Trust

Rest in God alone, my soul, for my hope comes from Him. He alone is my rock and my salvation, my stronghold; I will not be shaken. My salvation and glory depend on God; my strong rock, my refuge, is in God. Trust in Him at all times, you people; pour out your hearts before Him. God is our refuge. ~ Psalm 62:5–8

Your Walk

Therefore as you have received Christ Jesus the Lord, walk in Him, rooted and built up in Him and established in the faith, just as you were taught, and overflowing with thankfulness. ~ Colossians 2:6–7

Your Life from Here

Therefore, God's chosen ones, holy and loved, put on heartfelt compassion, kindness, humility, gentleness, and patience, accepting one another and forgiving one another if anyone has a complaint against another. Just as the Lord has forgiven you, so also you must forgive. Above all,

put on love—the perfect bond of unity.
~ Colossians 3:12–14

No Worries

Humble yourselves therefore under the mighty hand of God, so that He may exalt you in due time, casting all your care upon Him, because He cares for you. ~ 1 Peter 5:7

Quotes to Encourage You

Expect people to be better than they are; it helps them to become better. But don't be disappointed when they are not; it helps them to keep trying.~ Merry Browne

You are not wished riches, nor the glow of greatness, but that wherever you go, some weary heart will gladden into smiles, or that some shadowed life will know sunshine for a while. So, may your path be a track of light, like the blessing of an angel passing through the night. ~ Adapted from a church wall in England

*Every accomplishment starts with
the decision to try. ~ Author Unknown*

*Whatever the goal is that you want to win,
There's only one course and you have to begin,
For it's all in the starting and in giving your best.
That you find your own way to a life that is blessed.
So, step out in faith, go ahead, you can do it,
And God in His wisdom will help you walk through it!
~ Karen Moore*

*Those who long to be one with love achieve great things,
and shirk no effort. ~ Hadewijch*

*Don't worry about what you want, concentrate on what
you already have. ~ Author Unknown*

As you go forward . . .
Look up and not down,
Look forward and not back,
Look out and not in,
And lend a hand where you can.
~ Adapted from Edward Everett Hale

The longer I live the more I realize the impact of
attitude on life. Attitude to me is more important
than the past, than education, than money; than
circumstances, than failures, than success, than what
others think, or say, or do. I am convinced that life is
10% what happens to me and 90% how I react to it.
~ Chuck Swindoll

Your attitude, not your aptitude, will determine your
altitude. ~ Zig Ziglar

Prayer

Lord, thank You for being with me every step of the way, helping me get to where I am today, and guiding me into the future. Let me hold fast to all I know of You and shine Your precious light for others to see. Forgive me when I make poor choices or when I disappoint You in any way and bless me with opportunities to try again. Lord, help me to become worthy of You in every way and to embrace the work and the life plan You have for me. I praise Your name in love and gratitude. Amen.